T0300594

HELLO
BUGS

LAURENCE KING
First published in the United States in 2024
by Laurence King

ISBN 978-1-510-23050-7

10 9 8 7 6 5 4 3 2 1

Printed in China

MIX
Paper | Supporting
responsible forestry
FSC® C104740
www.fsc.org

Natural history consultants: Sarah Niemann and Derek Niemann

Laurence King
An imprint of
Hachette Children's Group
Part of Hodder and Stoughton
Carmelite House
50 Victoria Embankment
London EC4Y 0DZ

An Hachette UK Company
www.hachette.co.uk
www.hachettechildrens.co.uk
www.laurenceking.com

Nina Chakrabarti

HELLO
BUGS

A Little Guide to Nature

LAURENCE KING

CONTENTS

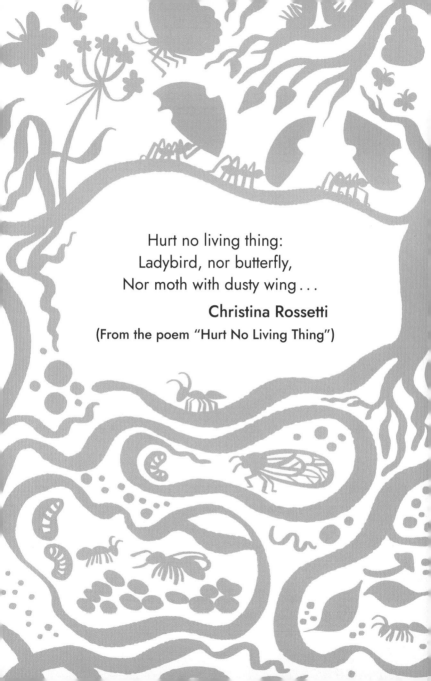

Hurt no living thing:
Ladybird, nor butterfly,
Nor moth with dusty wing...

Christina Rossetti
(From the poem "Hurt No Living Thing")

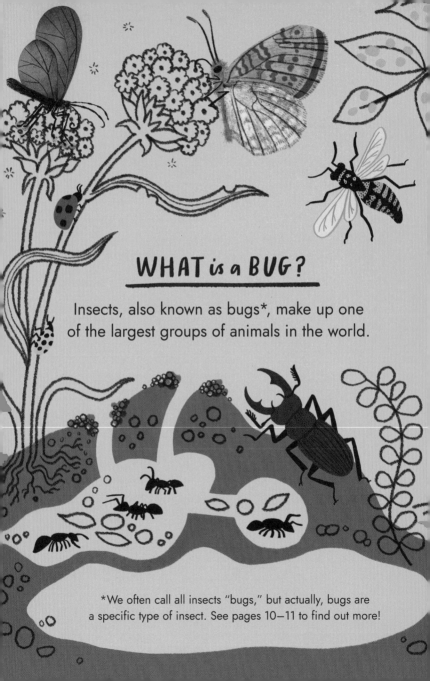

WHAT is a BUG?

Insects, also known as bugs*, make up one of the largest groups of animals in the world.

*We often call all insects "bugs," but actually, bugs are a specific type of insect. See pages 10–11 to find out more!

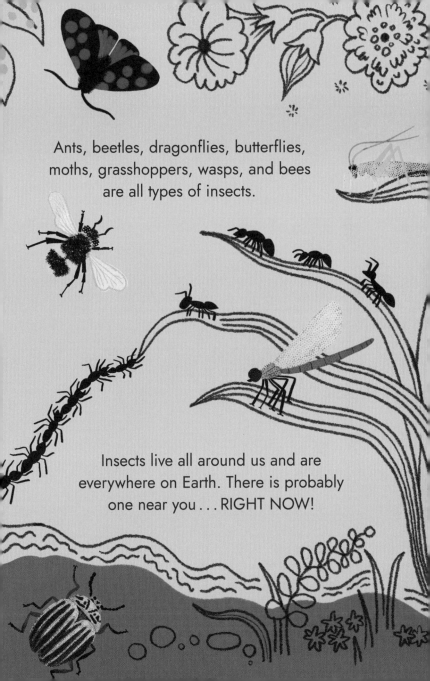

Ants, beetles, dragonflies, butterflies, moths, grasshoppers, wasps, and bees are all types of insects.

Insects live all around us and are everywhere on Earth. There is probably one near you . . . RIGHT NOW!

CREATURE FEATURES

Insects can look very different from one another,
but here are some things they have in common:

All insects have
six LEGS.

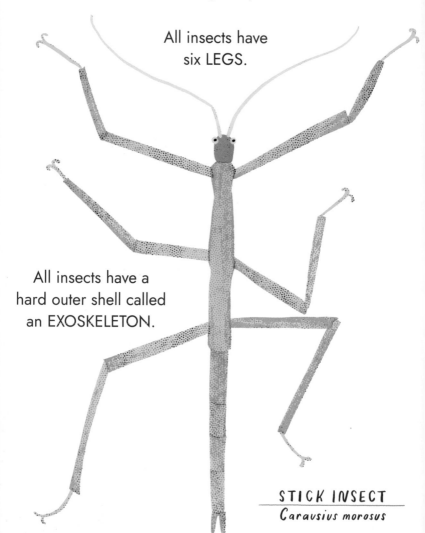

All insects have a
hard outer shell called
an EXOSKELETON.

STICK INSECT
Carausius morosus

All insects have three BODY parts:

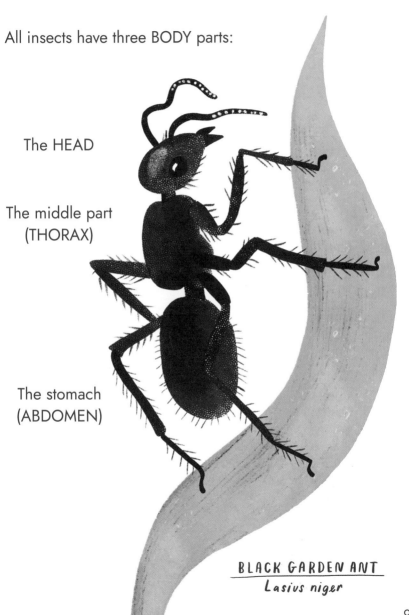

The HEAD

The middle part
(THORAX)

The stomach
(ABDOMEN)

BLACK GARDEN ANT
Lasius niger

9

TRUE BUGS

Scientists use the term *true bugs* to describe one particular group of insects. But don't let that bug you...

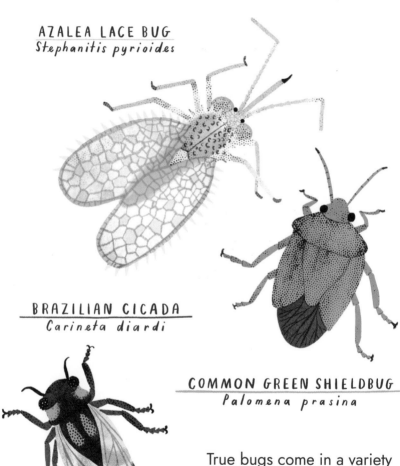

AZALEA LACE BUG
Stephanitis pyrioides

BRAZILIAN CICADA
Carineta diardi

COMMON GREEN SHIELDBUG
Palomena prasina

True bugs come in a variety of shapes and sizes and most have two sets of wings.

True bugs suck up sap from plants and blood from animals using its PROBOSCIS—a straw-like tube.

Aphids drink plant sap.

GREEN PEACH APHID
Myzus persicae

Bedbugs drink blood. Yikes!

COMMON BEDBUG
Cimex lectularius

Goodnight, sleep tight, don't let the bedbugs bite!

METAMORPHOSIS

Metamorphosis is a series of changes an insect goes through from egg to adult.

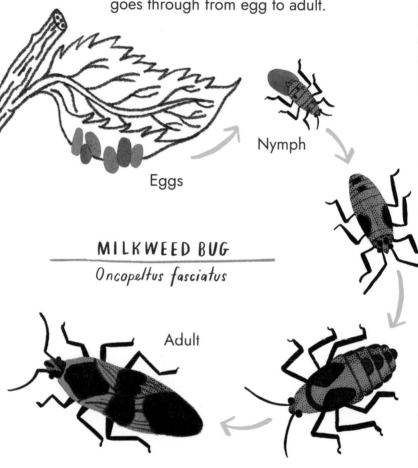

Eggs

Nymph

Adult

MILKWEED BUG
Oncopeltus fasciatus

Some young insects look like teeny tiny versions of the adult. They shed their skins, growing a little bigger each time. This is called "simple metamorphosis."

Other insects go through much bigger changes.
The young (larva) looks very different to the adult.
This is called "complete metamorphosis."

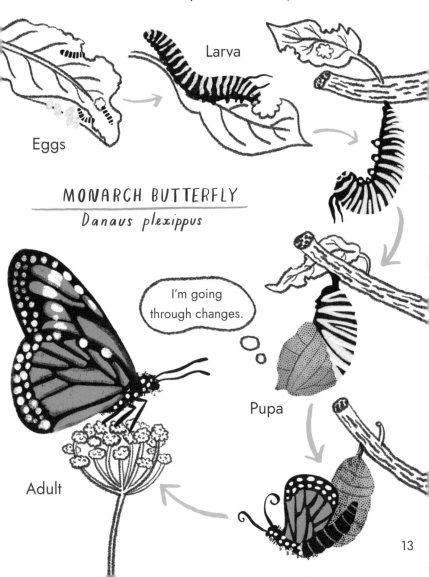

Larva

Eggs

MONARCH BUTTERFLY
Danaus plexippus

I'm going through changes.

Pupa

Adult

BEETLES

There are more species of beetles than any other insect on the planet. Perhaps you've seen one of these?

STAG BEETLE
Lucanus cervus

COMMON SEXTON BEETLE
Nicrophorus vespilloides

VIOLET CLICK BEETLE
Limoniscus violaceus

WASP BEETLE
Clytus arietis

GREEN TIGER BEETLE
Cicindela campestris

KNOTGRASS LEAF BEETLE
Chrysolina polita

ROSEMARY BEETLE
Chrysolina americana

JEWEL BEETLE
Chrysochroa fulgidissima

Beetles have two sets of wings: a pair of hard, protective outer wings and a soft inner set used for flying.

LADYBUGS

Ladybugs (also known as ladybirds) are a type of beetle.
Bright wing cases warn predators that they taste bad!

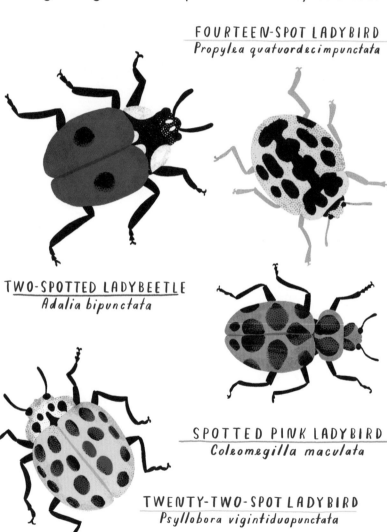

FOURTEEN-SPOT LADYBIRD
Propylea quatuordecimpunctata

TWO-SPOTTED LADYBEETLE
Adalia bipunctata

SPOTTED PINK LADYBIRD
Coleomegilla maculata

TWENTY-TWO-SPOT LADYBIRD
Psyllobora vigintiduopunctata

COLORADO POTATO BEETLE
Leptinotarsa decemlineata

Some ladybugs
have stripes . . .

. . . and lots and lots
have spots.

CONVERGENT LADYBEETLE
Hippodamia convergens

Others have amazing patterns.

FUNGUS-EATING LADYBIRD
Illeis galbula

Gardeners love most ladybugs because these little
bugs devour lots of plant-eating pests.

JUMPING BUGS

Grasshoppers, crickets, and katydids
are incredible high jumpers. Their
large hind legs act like catapults,
propelling them into the air.

COMMON GREEN GRASSHOPPER
Omocestus viridulus

Crickets are usually dark in color.
This helps them blend in with their
surroundings at night.

JUMPING BUSH CRICKET
Orocharis saltator

Katydids often hang out
on leaves—some even
look like them!

LEAF-MIMICKING KATYDID
Typophyllum bolivari

DRAGONFLY or DAMSELFLY?

Dragonflies and damselflies are related
and look very similar. But here's
how you can tell them apart:

EMPEROR DRAGONFLY
Anax imperator

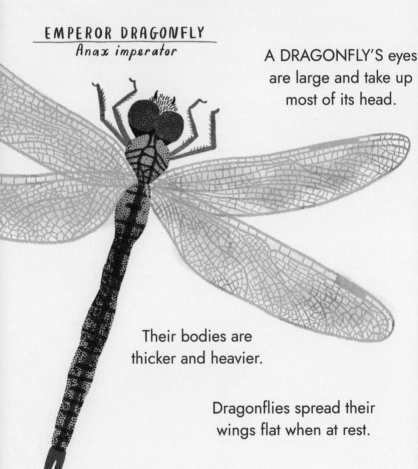

A DRAGONFLY'S eyes
are large and take up
most of its head.

Their bodies are
thicker and heavier.

Dragonflies spread their
wings flat when at rest.

Long before there were dinosaurs on Earth,
there were dragonflies gliding through the air.

Both damselflies and dragonflies are great at flying. They can flit around in any direction and hover in midair.

A DAMSELFLY'S eyes are smaller and are on each side of the insect's head.

Damselflies fold their wings when at rest.

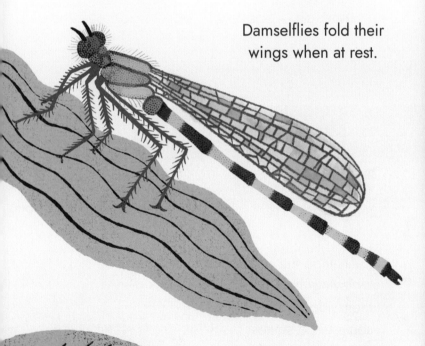

They have longer, thinner bodies.

COMMON BLUE DAMSELFLY
Enallagma cyathigerum

BUILD A BUG HOTEL

You will need:
* ✳ Empty plant pots
* ✳ Large stones
* ✳ Dead leaves, twigs, dried tree bark, and pine cones

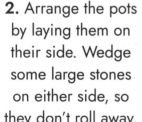

1. Wash and dry the plant pots.

2. Arrange the pots by laying them on their side. Wedge some large stones on either side, so they don't roll away.

3. Fill the "hotel rooms" with dried tree bark, dead leaves, pine cones, and twigs.

4. Make sure your materials are packed in tight, so that they stay put over winter.

There! You've made a cozy bug hotel that could host lots of hibernating insects during the colder months.

BUTTERFLY or MOTH?

It is always wonderful to spot a butterfly
or a moth, but can you tell them apart?

Most butterflies have
club-shaped antennae.

Butterflies have slender,
less hairy bodies.

PURPLE EMPEROR BUTTERFLY

Apatura iris

EMPEROR MOTH
Saturnia pavonia

Many moths have
feathery antennae.

Moths have thick,
furry bodies.

BUTTERFLY WINGS

These fluttering beauties use their colorful wings
to attract mates and warn off predators.

CLOUDED YELLOW
BUTTERFLY
Colias crocevs

PEACOCK
BUTTERFLY
Aglais io

MOURNING CLOAK
BUTTERFLY
Nymphalis antiopa

**ADONIS BLUE
BUTTERFLY**
Polyommatus bellargus

The wings of butterflies
and moths are made
from thousands of tiny,
shimmering scales.

**ALFALFA
BUTTERFLY**
Colias eurytheme

**COMMON GREEN BIRDWING
BUTTERFLY**
Ornithoptera priamus

MARVELOUS MOTHS

Most moths are nocturnal* and often dark-colored,
but many are active during the day. Daylight-loving moths
can be just as colorful as butterflies!

SIX-SPOT BURNET MOTH
Zygaena filipendulae

GARDEN TIGER MOTH
Arctia caja

ROSY MAPLE MOTH
Dryocampa rubicunda

*Active at night.

SPANISH MOON MOTH
Graellsia isabellae

PAINTED LICHEN MOTH
Hypoprepia fucosa

ELEPHANT HAWK-MOTH
Deilephila elpenor

Bright colors are a message to predators that the insect they are eyeing up might be poisonous!

SCARLET TIGER MOTH
Callimorpha dominula

29

BEE or WASP?

It's easy to confuse a bee with a wasp, but there are some differences. Here's how you can tell these buzzing bugs apart:

Bees have more rounded bodies.

Their bodies are covered in fuzzy yellow-and-black or orange-and-black bands.

HONEYBEE
Apis mellifera

Wasps have hairy heads but smooth, hairless bodies.

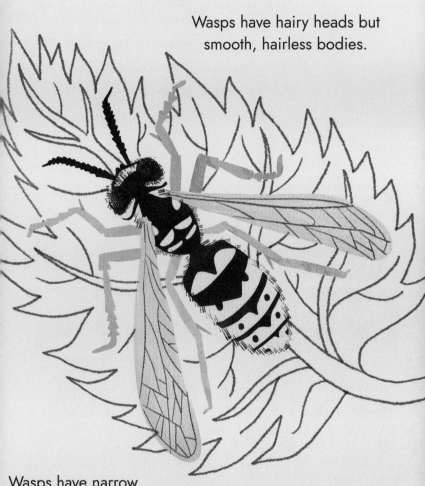

Wasps have narrow bodies and tiny nipped-in waists.

COMMON WASP
Vespula vulgaris

Wasps and bees are both helpful insects that pollinate plants.

LIFE in a BEEHIVE

In the wild, bees make their homes in wooded areas. Their nests, or hives, are full of busy bees, and each bee has its own job to do.

A beehive has just one QUEEN BEE. Her job is to lay eggs.

The queen is larger than the other bees and will live a longer life.

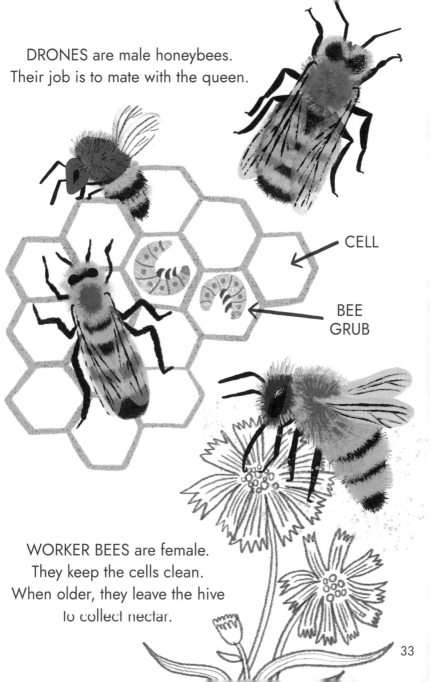

DRONES are male honeybees.
Their job is to mate with the queen.

CELL

BEE
GRUB

WORKER BEES are female.
They keep the cells clean.
When older, they leave the hive
to collect nectar.

FASCINATING ANTS

Ants can be found almost everywhere on Earth.
There are more than 12,000 known species!

CARPENTER ANTS
chew and make
tunnels in wood.

FIRE ANTS have extremely
strong jaws—a bite from
one can really hurt!

LEAF-CUTTER ANTS carry leaves to their nests.

ARGENTINE ANTS protect aphids. In return, the aphids produce a yummy liquid the ants love to eat.

SNIFF
SNIFF
SNIFF
SNIFF
SNIFF

Ants find food by following scent trails left by scout ants. These lone pioneers are sent out of the nest to find good things to eat.

LIFE in an ANT COLONY

Ants are sociable creatures that live in big nests called colonies. Ant society is very well organized. Each and every ant has a special job to do.

The QUEEN'S job is to lay eggs—lots and lots and LOTS of eggs.

EGGS

LARVAE

Ant colonies can have many tunnels and chambers.

WORKER ANTS are all female. Their job is to search for food and care for the young ants.

MALE ANTS exist just to mate with the queen. They die shortly after mating.

Really large ant colonies are called SUPER COLONIES. These super colonies can have hundreds of millions of members!

INTERESTING INSECTS

We hardly notice the tiny insects that live all around us, but they really are the most fascinating creatures.

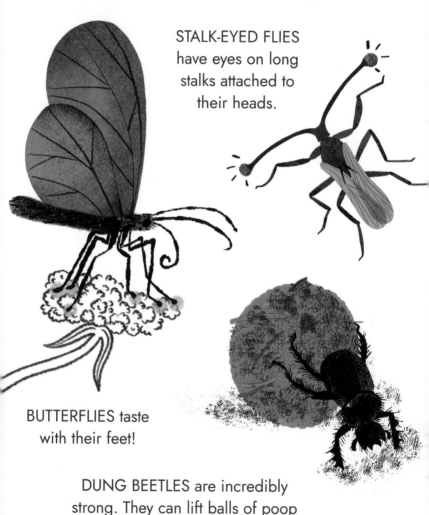

STALK-EYED FLIES have eyes on long stalks attached to their heads.

BUTTERFLIES taste with their feet!

DUNG BEETLES are incredibly strong. They can lift balls of poop many times heavier than they are!

DRAGONFLIES have almost 360-degree vision. This means that they can see above, below, and behind themselves all at once.

Insects can use their antennae to smell, taste, touch, feel vibrations, and sometimes even hear, too.

Some insects have ears in unusual places. Crickets have ears just below their knees!

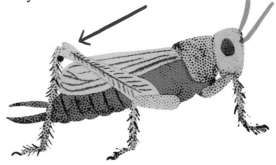

An ENTOMOLOGIST is someone who studies bugs. Could this be you one day?

LET'S GO BUG HUNTING!

A magnifying glass is not essential, but it can be handy for studying tiny bugs. The best time to go bug hunting is on a warm, sunny day.

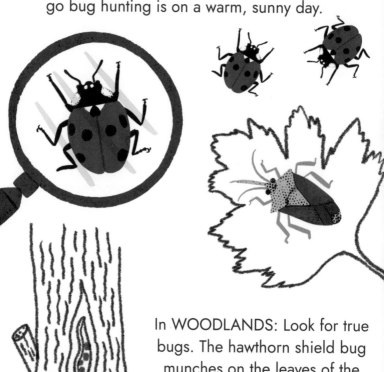

In WOODLANDS: Look for true bugs. The hawthorn shield bug munches on the leaves of the hawthorn tree.

Peek into cracks in trees and dead bark to see if you can spot any beetles.

Over LAKES or PONDS: Watch for dragonflies and damselflies darting across the water.

On SOIL: You might spot an ant or two hundred!

On FLOWERS: Observe bees, wasps, and butterflies.

On and under LEAVES: You might see ladybugs, aphids, and caterpillars.

In LONG GRASS: Look for grasshoppers and crickets.

CAMOUFLAGE and MIMICRY

Insects have many clever skills to find food and
keep themselves from becoming a meal for others!

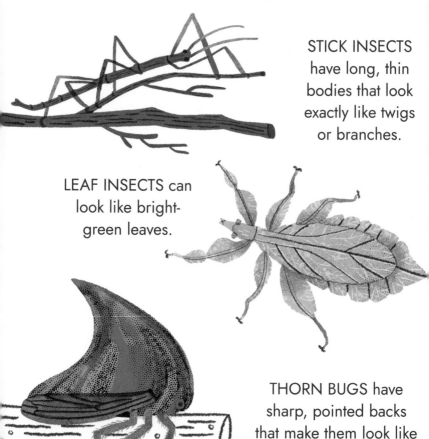

STICK INSECTS
have long, thin
bodies that look
exactly like twigs
or branches.

LEAF INSECTS can
look like bright-
green leaves.

THORN BUGS have
sharp, pointed backs
that make them look like
a thorn on a plant.

Camouflage means using colors, patterns, and shapes
to blend in with the surroundings.

SPIDER MOTHS have markings on their wings that make them look like spiders with spindly legs!

FLOWER MANTISES imitate flowers so they can eat the eager insects that visit to drink their nectar.

Hello, you!

OWL BUTTERFLIES have large spots on their wings that look like owl eyes.

Mimicry is where one species makes itself look like another to frighten off predators or attract prey.

GLOW-in-the-DARK BUGS

Some insects produce their own light at night to advertise to potential mates, scare off predators, or to attract prey.

GLOWWORM
Lampyris noctiluca

ADULT

LARVA

CALIFORNIA PINK GLOWWORM
Microphotus angustus

NEW ZEALAND GLOWWORM
Arachnocampa luminosa

HEADLIGHT BEETLE
Pyrophorus nyctophanus

RAILROAD WORM
Phrixothrix hirtus

BUGS in FOLKLORE

Throughout history, we humans have been fascinated by the tiny creatures that live alongside us.

Scarab beetle jewelry was a symbol of rebirth and was buried with the dead in ancient EGYPT.

In ancient GREECE, bees represented Artemis, the goddess of hunting and wild nature.

The Hopi people of NORTH AMERICA perform a thanksgiving dance after harvest. It is called the butterfly dance.

Kaggen is a shape-shifting folk hero for the San people of SOUTH AFRICA. He often takes the form of a praying mantis.

Before it was called the Land of the Rising Sun, JAPAN was known as Akitsushima, meaning "Island of the Dragonfly."

According to VIKING legend, the god Thor sent the ladybug to Earth riding on a lightning bolt.

BE A FRIEND TO BUGS

1. Grow flowers in your yard or on your window ledge to attract bees and butterflies.

2. Find out which butterflies live near you, and grow the plants that they like to visit.

3. Place a log or pile of leaves in the back of the yard to provide shelter for beetles.

4. Let a part of your yard go wild. Sow wildflower seeds, and watch insects flock there.

5. Ask your teacher if you could build a bug hotel (see pages 22–23) on the school grounds as a class project.

6. Do not touch or hurt bugs. Most insects we encounter do not mean us any harm—they are leading rich, extraordinary lives of their own.